Aunty Cake

written and illustrated by

Ros Asquith

OXFORD
UNIVERSITY PRESS
AUSTRALIA & NEW ZEALAND

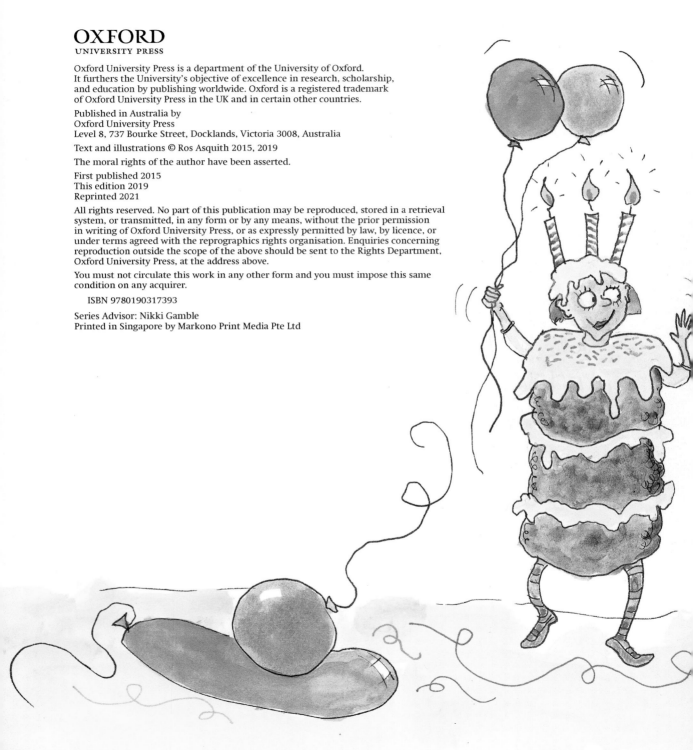

OXFORD
UNIVERSITY PRESS

Oxford University Press is a department of the University of Oxford.
It furthers the University's objective of excellence in research, scholarship,
and education by publishing worldwide. Oxford is a registered trademark
of Oxford University Press in the UK and in certain other countries.

Published in Australia by
Oxford University Press
Level 8, 737 Bourke Street, Docklands, Victoria 3008, Australia

Text and illustrations © Ros Asquith 2015, 2019

The moral rights of the author have been asserted.

First published 2015
This edition 2019
Reprinted 2021

ISBN 9780190317393

Series Advisor: Nikki Gamble
Printed in Singapore by Markono Print Media Pte Ltd

Aunty Cake **loved** having parties.

You may be wondering why she was called
Aunty Cake. Perhaps she looked like a cake?

Well, no. Look:

it was because of her
wonderful cakes!

Aunty Cake baked delicious cakes. She was
also very kind – and very, *very* forgetful!

On Monday, it was cold but she forgot
her hat and her gloves.

Tuesday was wet but she *couldn't* find her umbrella.

On windy Wednesday, she could not see her scarf anywhere.

The rain on Thursday was terrible. It was cold and the wind was howling. Poor Aunty Cake couldn't find

her umbrella,

her scarf

or

her gloves!

But she *did* have her hat!

The wind blew her hat along the street, over
the hedge, into the park, and up into a cherry tree.

whoosh!

Please
don't pick
the fruit.

Aunty Cake shook the branches
of the tree. Ripe cherries tumbled
down all over her.

The cherries fell into her
pockets and hung from
her buttons. When at
last her hat came down,
it looked quite
amazing!

Plip Plop

9

"Please **don't** pick the fruit!" a stern voice growled.

"Oh," said Aunty Cake. "I wasn't. It's just that the wind …

my hat …

the cherries …"

The police officer didn't let her explain.

"What is your name and address?" she asked.

"My name is Aunty Cake." But Aunty Cake was so flustered that she forgot her address.

A crowd gathered.

"Aunty Cake! That's not a proper
name," said a girl in pearls.

"She's a cherry thief!" shouted
a mean lady in green.

Poor Aunty Cake said nothing.

"No! Wait!" called out a small boy with a big smile. "She is Aunty Cake. And she wouldn't steal anything! She *gives* things to people. She even makes the cakes for our football matches!"

"If Aunty Cake is a thief, then I am a *penguin*," joked the boy's dad.

"Oh, really? Sorry, madam," said the police officer.

Aunty Cake followed the boy and his dad.
"Thank you very much," she said. "I don't think I know you, do I?"

"Yes, have you forgotten?" said the small boy with the big smile. "You used to read stories to me when I was in hospital. And you help the children in the school where my mum teaches."

"We've often seen you planting flowers in the park," his dad added.

"Oh, yes! That's me!" chuckled Aunty Cake.
"But I'm afraid I'm rather bad at remembering faces.
Sometimes I get a bit of a surprise when I see my
own face in the mirror!"

At this, the boy's big smile turned into

a huge happy laugh.

The next day was Friday.
It was fine and sunny.

Aunty Cake wore her
hat and scarf, and popped
her gloves in her pocket ...
just in case!

She was dreaming about
an idea for a party.

She went to the market
and filled her basket with
cherries. Next, she bought
a **mountain** of strawberries.
But she had forgotten
her other basket! So she
filled her hat with the strawberries
and set off for home.

On the way home, she bumped into the
police officer. It was the very same one!

"Caught red-handed!"
the police officer said. Holding all
that fruit had given Aunty Cake
very red hands ...
 ... but that wasn't what
the police officer meant.

"I'm not a thief!" said Aunty Cake. "I paid for all that fruit. Here is the receipt to prove it."

But she had forgotten the receipt!

Aunty Cake looked around and saw the girl in pearls and the mean lady in green.

"You've done it *again*!" they moaned.

Poor Aunty Cake. All she wanted to do was bake!

"I *bought* the cherries and the strawberries," she gulped. "Ask the lady at the market! She'll tell you that I paid for them."

A tear ran down her cheek, but of course, she had forgotten her hanky.

Just then, the boy with the big smile ran up.

He was waving something.

It was the **receipt!**

The mean lady in green muttered, "Sorry," and gave Aunty Cake a tissue.

The girl in pearls blushed.

The police officer scribbled out the notes in her notebook.

"We were wrong, I can see," she admitted. "We all owe you an apology."

"Oh, that's all right," smiled Aunty Cake. "Please, let's start again. Come to my house for a party this evening."

So they all went to Aunty Cake's party. They ate cherry cake and strawberry shortbread, and swapped stories about being forgetful.

And none of them ever forgot the kind Aunty Cake – or her wonderful, delicious cakes!